Original title:
Petal-Painted Pages

Copyright © 2025 Creative Arts Management OÜ
All rights reserved.

Author: Jameson Hartfield
ISBN HARDBACK: 978-1-80566-720-9
ISBN PAPERBACK: 978-1-80566-849-7

Calligraphy of Colorful Blooms

In gardens bright, the colors clash,
A daisy says, "I'm quite the brash!"
The roses giggle, the tulips tease,
"You only stand because you're on your knees!"

The violets smirk, in hues so bold,
"Watch the pansies, they're getting old!"
A daffodil chuckles at daisies spry,
"Don't fret, my friend, we bloom and die!"

Nature's Wisdom on Warm Pages

In sunshine beams, the wisdom flows,
A whispering breeze in the garden grows.
"Today I'll nap, tomorrow I'll wine,"
Said the old oak tree, "That's my design!"

A squirrel chimes in, with a nutty tale,
"Chasing the bees? You'll surely fail!"
Leaves laugh aloud, as the clouds roll by,
"Gravity's silly, just watch us fly!"

Musings Among the Verdant Verses

In emerald fields where giggles sway,
A dandelion jokes, "I'm here to stay!"
"Blow me away? Oh, do your best,
I'm back in spring, as a fearless guest!"

The grass blurted out, with a hefty grin,
"I've heard that joke, let's sing again!"
They hummed a tune, full of silly glee,
As butterflies danced, oh what a spree!

A Garden of Infinite Ink

With petals dipped in ink's embrace,
The flowers scribble, leaving no trace.
A lilac thought, "What's all the fuss?
My scent is gold, but your puns are rust!"

A sunflower winked, with a jolly flair,
"Make way for me, I'm the fairest heir!"
Yet all around, the laughter spread,
As every bloom imagined what lay ahead!

The Language of Leaves and Ink

In a garden where jokes sprout wide,
Leaves giggle, and the flowers collide.
A page turned with a rustle and cheer,
Whispers of laughter drift through the year.

The daisies are gossiping, can you hear?
Tales of the sun and a pesky deer.
Ink from the fountain, a splash on the grass,
Lies of the squirrels, oh what a class!

When autumn talks, it's all in jest,
Witty exchanges from tree to nest.
The maple chuckles, the oak gives a wink,
Turning stories into shades as they shrink.

On these vibrant sheets, joy's all around,
Each scribbled line holds laughter profound.
So grab a branch, dip it in lore,
Let the leaves tell tales, forevermore!

Fragments of Petal Dreams

In a garden where flowers play,
They gossip about bees all day.
One rose claimed she tried to fly,
But only ended with a sigh.

The daisies laughed, they danced so free,
While violets sipped their herbal tea.
A dandelion wore a crown of glee,
Dreams of fluff set wild and free.

Tulips bragged of morning dew,
"What's your secret?" said the blue.
They winked and murmured, full of jest,
"Just drink it up—it's quite the best!"

In this garden, every bloom,
Sows laughter, joy, and sweet perfume.
With petals bright, they spin their tales,
In one big laugh, their humor sails.

Stories Inked in Flora

A daisy wrote a playful book,
Of every leaf and little nook.
With ink of dew and laughter's sound,
Stories of bees and fun abound.

The tulip shared some juicy gossip,
About a snail who loved to frolic.
Her secret? She slid with grace,
No trace was left in this wild place!

A fern recounted days of rain,
When puddles turned to dancing lanes.
With every splash that made them cheer,
They twirled in joy, without a fear.

In the garden, stories meld,
With every bloom and drop upheld.
They pen a world so full of zest,
Where every petal knows best!

Written in the Garden's Embrace

In a nook where sunflowers grin,
Chill laughter bounces—let's begin!
A bumblebee told silly puns,
While laughing daisies rolled in runs.

The violets hosted a tea time,
With petals crisp, it was sublime.
The roses argued who brewed best,
"Just smell the cup," they jested, blessed!

In whispers soft, the stories grew,
Of tiny bugs in endless view.
Their antics made the leaves all sway,
In this garden of whimsy play.

So grab a seat among the flowers,
Where laughter blooms for endless hours.
In petals soft, the tales are spun,
In this embrace, we find the fun!

Floral Fragments of Memory

A memory tucked in lavender's hue,
A frolicsome tale, so sweet and true.
The poppies giggled at clouds of fluff,
While sprinkling pollen in a puff!

The lilacs swayed, their laughter loud,
As squirrels donned hats, oh what a crowd!
With acorns shared, there's never a frown,
In this whimsical floral town.

The orchids whispered secrets at night,
Of fireflies dancing in sheer delight.
With each twinkle, a wish takes flight,
A memory spun in soft moonlight.

So here's to blooms that tickle the mind,
With every giggle, pure joy we find.
In floral fragments, laughter grows,
In every petal, the fun just flows!

Verses Stitched with Stamen Thread

In a garden where rhymes grow,
Silly bees dance with a flow.
Chasing words like honey sweet,
They twirl around on their little feet.

A butterfly lost its way,
Decided to join in the play.
It tripped on a line from a rhyme,
And turned it into a silly mime.

Tulips giggle as they sway,
Waving at clouds that drift away.
With every verse, they toss and tease,
Making pollen jokes in the breeze.

When roses burst with laughter loud,
They cover up the modest crowd.
Every rhyme sung in flowery cheer,
Brings smiles to all who venture here.

Poetry Drenched in Floral Dew

Mornings bloom with giggles bright,
Dewdrops giggle in morning light.
They tumble down from leaves with glee,
Falling into verses, wild and free.

The daisies sport a charming hat,
And engage in a cheeky spat.
Who wrote the line about the bees?
Oh dear, it's just a silly tease!

Lilies nod in rhythmic time,
Chanting softly in floral rhyme.
Their petals wave, they play tag all day,
Mocking the sun in a playful way.

An acorn wanders without a care,
To hear the flowers share their dare.
With each dropped line, the laughter grows,
As blooms compose their merry prose.

The Scent of Inked Blossom Narratives

In a field where stories sprout,
Dandelions twist, dance about.
With ink in hand, they scribble new,
Planting tales in fragrant dew.

A daffodil pens a jolly tale,
About a snail who rode a whale.
With a plot so wild, it twists and turns,
And earned the blooms' delightful churns.

The violets hum a tiny tune,
Teasing the stars that shone by noon.
They paint a world with all their might,
Turning garden life into pure delight.

As petals flutter like pages turned,
Each story shared leaves laughter burned.
In flowers' whispers, secrets blend,
Where every giggle finds its end.

A Symphony of Flora and Verse

The chorus blooms in sun-kissed cheer,
With lilacs strumming songs we hear.
Daisies hop on beat with flair,
While roses punch lines in the air.

A marigold starts a quirky rhyme,
Tickling bees all day in time.
With every buzz, a giggle grows,
As petals bloom in wondrous flows.

A serenade of colors bright,
In every crevice, pure delight.
With verses sprouting from the ground,
Where nature's humor knows no bound.

So join the dance in flowery dreams,
In gardens laced with laughter's schemes.
As blooms unite in joyous fun,
A symphony for everyone.

The Soul of Spring in Ink

In a garden where words bloom,
Funny things lift the gloom.
A daisy wrote a letter bright,
Saying, 'Sneeze with all your might!'

A rose declared it was quite a tease,
To dance about in summer breeze.
Each petal chuckled, full of glee,
Sipping nectar, oh so free!

The ink spilled over, what a sight,
Flamingos in tuxedos, oh so bright!
The bees buzzed with the latest news,
While ants wore hats and shiny shoes.

But what's that? A daffodil's shout!
"Who left the door open? I'm out!"
In boxes of laughter, we stampede,
With every note, our hearts proceed!

Letters from the Leafy Realm

From leafy lanes, the letters flow,
A cabbage writes, 'I'm quite the show!'
A snail sent notes in slow, smooth curls,
While kittens chased butterflies and twirls.

"I'm rad-ish," said the veggie crew,
"Writing nonsense, just for you!"
Lettuce laughed in its leafy bed,
Chasing dreams from its veggie head.

The bookworms read of clouds that wink,
As the carrots giggled, 'Time to shrink!'
On each page, a funny quip,
With veggie jokes, they let it rip!

So open a letter from the ground,
In every word, pure joy is found.
In leafy realms, the humor's grand,
With each bright letter, take a stand!

Reflections in Botanical Ink

With ink made from the sunlit dew,
A tulip wrote, "I dream of you!"
Reflections dance on the pond's glass,
While frogs in tuxedos watch the sass.

"Don't lily-pad to the wrong tune,"
Chortled the blooms under the moon.
A daffodil burst with laughter loud,
As ants paraded, so very proud.

"Hey there, cool cat," the roses grin,
"Let's write a story with a spin!"
A bumblebee chimed in with flair,
"Why is it that you don't share hair?"

In botanical glory, the fun's not scarce,
With jotted notes doing their dance and prance.
For every line is a merry wink,
In the world where flowers all ink and think!

A Quilted Tale of Blossoms

A quilt spun from brightly stitched blooms,
Held tales of laughter, sunny perfumes.
A sunflower joked, "I'm the fairest!"
While daisies shouted, "No one can bare us!"

With needle and thread, they crafted fun,
As giggles burst bright like the sun.
"Who took the last drop of juice?" they teased,
While bumblebees buzzed, thoroughly amused.

An iris chimed, "I'll tell a tale,
Of roses who forgot their veil!"
The petals shook in laughter wide,
Under the moon, they bloomed with pride.

So come and snuggle in this patch,
Where every stitch is a joyous match.
In quilters' corners, the stories sway,
And laughter blooms at the end of the day!

Secrets Between the Flowered Lines

In gardens where the rumors grow,
Bees tell tales, and daisies know.
Tulips whisper secrets bold,
While pansies giggle, never cold.

The roses plot with a cheeky grin,
Deciding who will take the win.
A dandelion pranks in the sun,
'Hey, look at me, I'm a lot of fun!'

The violets hide with mischievous glee,
As a caterpillar spills his tea.
Sunflowers strike poses and pose some more,
Can you believe what's in store?

So gather 'round for laughs and cheer,
Nature's jokes are always near.
In every sprout, a story sways,
Among these flowers, life's a play!

Petaled Poetry and Whispered Wishes

Leaves rustle with a giggly sound,
As petals swirl, joy is found.
Haikus bounce from bloom to bloom,
With rhymes that make the craziest loom.

The lilacs plot an evening show,
Inviting friends with a vibrant glow.
A sunflower's wink can sway a breeze,
While crickets dance with silly ease.

Daisies have a game of tag,
While bumblebees do a little brag.
Lavender laughs, her scent a tease,
A perfume that sets the world at ease.

When petals write, oh what a scene,
With witty lines and shades of green.
So come, take part, in this quirky play,
A flower's fun in every way!

Blossoms that Breathe in Stanzas

Inhale the laughter from every bloom,
As blossoms burst from winter's gloom.
Narcissus dreams with a wink so sly,
While tulips bubble as days go by.

A daffodil's jibe can crack a smile,
With petals dancing all the while.
The gardens hold a parade each day,
With violets showing off in a play.

A lily jests with a twirl and spin,
While the pansies plot a playful grin.
Lavish hues in every hue,
Each petal whispers "Look at you!"

So let's embark on this floral spree,
With stanzas blooming, wild and free.
In this joyful place where laughter flies,
The blossoms breathe, beneath the skies!

A Canvas of Colors in Written Form

Here lies a canvas lush and bright,
With colors dancing, quite the sight.
Crayons made from sun and rain,
Sketching tales that can entertain!

Magenta marigolds spin a yarn,
While golden blooms keep up the charm.
With every stroke, they tease and poke,
Creating laughter, their favorite joke!

The bluebells giggle, "Oh dear me!
Shall we hold a flower jamboree?"
With petals as dance partners in flight,
Under the beams of heavens' light.

For every color scribbles a tale,
Of bees on holiday, and wind in sail.
A fun-filled poem, fresh and warm,
In a garden of giggles, we gather 'round and swarm!

Palette of Nature's Prose

In gardens bright with hues so fair,
A tulip winks, 'I caught a bear!'
The daisies giggle, and bumblebees hum,
As nature's colors dance and run.

With every shade, a story spun,
A daffodil dreams of having fun.
While violets whisper secrets sweet,
With petals soft beneath our feet.

Petunias twirl in a floral ballet,
While sunflowers grin at another day.
Chasing rainbows, we laugh and play,
In this whimsical, flowery fray.

Beneath the sky, let laughter bloom,
Where every bud holds a playful room.
The palette swirls, the laughter sways,
As we paint our lives in sunny rays.

Echoes in the Flowered Journal

In grassy fields where flowers speak,
A daisy jokes, 'Do I look sleek?'
The marigolds wink, sharing a laugh,
As bees buzz by to join the gaff.

Each bloom, a quirk, a tale to tell,
A rose confesses it sings quite well.
With petals ripe for gossip and cheer,
They whisper jokes for all to hear.

Tulips strut in their vibrant hats,
While dandelions play with curious cats.
These echoes flit on the gentle breeze,
With all of nature, as they please.

Let petals rhyme with chuckles and grins,
In this garden where laughter begins.
Nature's script is filled with pure fun,
As we bask beneath the playful sun.

Vignettes Among the Blossoms

With blossoms bold, the antics start,
A sunflower farts, that's quite the art!
The lilacs giggle, rolling with glee,
While butterflies dance, wild and free.

Petals tell tales, each more absurd,
Like zany bees that cannot be heard.
A lily claims it's a ninja at night,
Only to trip on its own delight.

Roses in hats, prancing along,
Join violets in a risqué song.
With breezes tickling on winter's thread,
These vignettes bloom where laughter's spread.

In the floral pews, where humor reigns,
The palettes burst with silly gains.
A comedic world of blossom and cheer,
Brings smiles to all who venture near.

The Blooming Chronicles

In the chronicles where flowers dwell,
A clumsy bee fell into a shell.
The roses chuckle at his buzzing spree,
As daisies mock, 'What's wrong, dear bee?'

The garden hosts a fashion show,
Where blooms compete on a runway glow.
Sunflowers strut, with stems held high,
While chubby daisies dance and sigh.

With every petal, a laugh unfurls,
As snapdragons snap, giving silly swirls.
The blooms unite for a comedy act,
Where laughter is bright and humor is packed.

In this tale of petals, joy's the theme,
Where nature scribbles its funny dream.
So join the fun in this floral land,
And let all hearts bloom, hand in hand.

Petals Beneath the Written Sky

Beneath the vast and silly sky,
Daisies dance as words fly by.
A tulip trips on a pun,
As laughter blooms, oh what fun!

Giggling leaves with tales to spin,
In this garden, jokes can win.
Roses tease with a wink and nod,
While daisies laugh, this isn't odd.

Each flower shares a goofy line,
Telling stories of the divine.
Sunflowers grin, they're in on it,
Join the bloom for a comedy skit!

So grab your seeds, plant some cheer,
Let every petal spread the gear.
With humor sprouting from the ground,
In this flower field, joy is found!

Blossoms in the Book of Life.

In the pages where humor grows,
Blossoms tell all their funny woes.
A rose complains, its thorns are tough,
A daisy giggles, saying 'that's enough!'

Butterflies read, all in a flutter,
Wings whisper tales, it makes them mutter.
Every blossom has a joke to share,
Floral punchlines float in the air.

The sunbeam bursts in a cheeky grin,
Spilling laughter, let's all dive in!
While bees buzz with a giggly hum,
In this floral tale, we all succumb.

Jokes unfold like buds at dawn,
A blossom's wit, a marigold's brawn.
Turn the pages, come take a look,
This book of life is quite the nook!

Whispers of Blossom Ink

With ink made out of fragrant blooms,
Stories sprout from garden rooms.
A lilac quips with a comic twist,
While violets giggle, not to be missed.

Bumblebees buzzing a hearty laugh,
Ivy vines drafting a flowery half.
Petals scribed with humorous strokes,
Jokesters hidden among the oaks.

The ink spills out on each leafy page,
Scripted stories unleash the sage.
Forget the sad and embrace the quirk,
Floral whispers, they do all the work!

So read aloud under sunny rays,
As flowers pen out their funny ways.
Each verse a giggle, each line a cheer,
In this garden, the laughter's clear!

Fragments of a Floral Diary

In this diary where blooms confess,
Each flower's tale is a funny mess.
A daffodil slips while telling a tale,
Laughs so hard it hijacks the mail.

Petals scribble in colorful tones,
While tulips giggle and lose their phones.
Every leaf tells a story grand,
With laughs sprouting from the land.

Vases filled with gags on repeat,
Where all the flowers gather to greet.
Chortles echo through the fragrant night,
In this luggage of laughter, hold on tight!

So join the fun, don't be shy,
In this fruity fondant of a floral sky.
Grab a petal and read along,
In a garden full of joke and song!

Blossoms Entwined with Memory

A daisy danced with the past's embrace,
　Twirling in tales of a friendly race.
Laughter echoed where petals once lay,
　Tickling the thoughts that never decay.

The rose had a secret, it whispered so sly,
　'Why don't daisies wear hats? Oh my!'
Buttercups giggled, but soon all agreed,
　Wearing a hat is a flower's fine creed.

In the garden, a party, oh what a sight,
With bees doing ballet under the moonlight.
Tulips were judging the daisies' new shoes,
While cheerful sunflowers exchanged all the news.

Memories tangled in vines of delight,
Each bloom cracking jokes, all flowers polite.
With laughter in petals and joy in their lanes,
　Nature's sweet tales quirkily reign.

Verses Beneath a Canopy of Blooms

Under a canopy of colors so bright,
Bumblebees buzzed with pure delight.
Lilacs recited rhymes in the breeze,
Zinnias chuckled, 'We're the bees' knees!'

A sunflower sighed, 'I can't take the heat!'
'Why do we always have to be sweet?'
Pansies shrugged with a colorful flair,
'Let's wear polka dots if you dare!'

Daffodils debated the best shade of gold,
With tulips insisting they were quite bold.
In this garden of giggles and hues so divine,
Each flower found humor beneath the sunshine.

They planned a parade with a musical tune,
Where petals would waltz as a flower-crowned boon.
Oh to be part of such whimsical sights,
Under a sky filled with floral delights!

Scribbled Secrets of the Green Page

On pages of green, stories unfold,
With scribbles and sketches; oh, how bold!
Ladybugs laughing, they read with delight,
'That plant's got style, what a sight!'

A creeping vine whispered, 'Here's my prank!'
Twisting around like a cheeky tank.
The ferns were snickering over a shroom,
'Be careful, he's got quite a big room!'

Gnarled trees pondered their ages in fun,
Playing charades with the setting sun.
Each leaf a giggle, each branch a jest,
This green page's party was simply the best!

They penned a new tale on the breeze's sweet air,
With humor in leaves and laughter to share.
Nature wrote on, with each tiny twist,
In a book of delight no one could resist!

An Ode to Nature's Written Touch

In a garden where laughter's the finest prose,
Nature composes with petals that glow.
A clumsy bumblebee bumped into a rose,
'Excuse me, dear flower, I'm trying to doze!'

The wind penned a sonnet for all to admire,
About a shy bloom who dreamt of a choir.
With each little breeze, the leaves made a tune,
As daisies hummed softly beneath the bright moon.

Chirping crickets joined in the fun,
While mushrooms—oh, dear—risked a frolic or run.
Together they danced in a whimsical spree,
Nature's own narrative, oh, what a glee!

With ink made of dew and a brush made of light,
The flowers wrote stories, all colorful and bright.
In this funny fable, where all blooms belong,
Nature's sweet laughter forever stays strong.

Inked Petals of Remembrance

In a garden full of giggles,
I lost my favorite pen.
The flowers, they were snickering,
As I searched again and again.

The daisies held my secrets,
With petals full of glee.
They whispered all my stories,
To the humble bumblebee.

The sunflowers were suspicious,
With grins upon their face.
They promised to keep quiet,
But I knew they'd leave a trace.

So I inked my heart on blossoms,
As bees buzzed with delight.
The pages were alive with laughter,
In colorful morning light.

The Colorful Chronicles of the Meadow

Once a crocus told a tale,
Of how the grass was green.
A butterfly chimed in with flair,
"But I was the one seen!"

A primrose winked at daffodils,
"We're the best dressed here!"
They twirled and danced in sunshine spills,
Proclaiming 'We've no fear!'

Chasing shadows, giggling loud,
The violets made a fuss.
With colors bright, they drew a crowd,
And all the bees took buses!

The sun began to slowly set,
With hues of pink and gold.
The flowers shared the laughter yet,
In stories yet untold.

Quatrains of Blossoming Hearts

A lily laughed at morning dew,
"It's just a splash and run!"
A tangled rose replied anew,
"I bloom to have some fun!"

The tulips twirled in dizzy spins,
And giggled with a breeze.
They told each other silly sins,
In whispers through the trees.

Dandelions in a row,
Wrote poems on the air.
Their fluffy heads, a comic show,
Took laughs without a care.

As night rolled in with velvet skies,
The stars began to wink.
A chorus of sweet flower sighs,
Made every heart rethink.

Blooms in the Margins of Memory

In a notebook, bright and quirky,
The roses scribbled jokes.
They cracked up till they turned all murky,
And tickled all the folks.

The pansies painted silly scenes,
With crayons on the grass.
They giggled at their wobbly greens,
And fully filled each class.

A sunflower caught a breeze,
And said, "I'm quite the star!"
While lilacs danced and tried to tease,
"You're just a tall bizarre!"

They filled the margins with their glee,
In all their colored joy.
With every line, they'd shout with glee,
Creating tales to buoy.

The Artistry of Plant-Laced Words

In the garden of chatter, we plant our seeds,
With rhymes that flutter like whimsical weeds.
A daisy snickers, a rose cracks a smile,
While sunflowers gossip in a flowery style.

Each line a leaf, each word a vine,
Twining around tales, oh how they shine!
We scribble our stories in pollen and mirth,
Crafting a world where laughter gives birth.

Bees buzz around, adding notes of their own,
Mixing up stanzas, like honey they've grown.
With each twist and turn on this floral escapade,
Life's garden of humor, in words, is portrayed.

A Bouquet of Verse and Whisper

Gathering giggles in blooms of delight,
I'll trade you a pun for a petal so bright.
Tulips tease daisies with jokes rare and spry,
Pansies throw shade while they all laugh and sigh.

This bouquet of silliness, an odd little bunch,
Ties laughter in ribbons like a sweet crunchy lunch.
With a stem full of whimsy and leaves made of cheer,
Each verse is a bloom that draws friends ever near.

Lavender giggles, while ivy entwines,
Crafting snickers and chuckles in floral designs.
Oh, the silliness dances, as nature's art sways,
Like puns sprinkled softly in sunshine's warm rays.

Vignettes of Nature Enlivened

Once in a garden where jokes start to sprout,
A tulip told tales, and the daisies all clout.
"Why did the flower refuse to share tea?"
"Because it was too rooted!" they laughed with great glee.

Across the green expanse, gaily breezes would weave,
A symphony of laughter, you'd think it deceives.
The daisies in tandem would spin, and they'd twirl,
Whispering secrets that made petals unfurl.

With each fragrant flip, humor began to bloom,
As bees joined the banquet, bringing friends to the room.
Nature's sweet verses play tricks on the ear,
Painting vignettes of joy, spreading fun far and near.

The Floral Syntax of a Wandering Soul

A wandering wordsmith finds joy in the green,
Where daisies do cartwheels, their laughter a scene.
They scribble sweet verses as flowers prance by,
With humor spun gently from roots deep and spry.

In this syntax of petals, our stories collide,
A comedy rooted where wild things reside.
Chortles of blooms move like waves on the breeze,
Each line a giggle, like honey from bees.

"Why do the roses wear such a frown?"
"Oh, thorns can be funny when they come to town!"
With every giggle, the garden rejoices,
In this floral assembly, we're blending our voices.

Silken Words on Spring's Canvas

In springtime's winks, the jokes unfold,
Silly blooms giggle, their stories bold.
A daisy loses its hat in the breeze,
While tulips charade, putting minds at ease.

Daffodils dance with a ticklish cheer,
Sneezing petals, oh dear, oh dear!
A rose cracks jokes, its thorns hold tight,
While sunflowers spin tales of day and night.

Bees laugh along with their buzzing sounds,
As rhymes take flight from upturned grounds.
With pollen fizz and garden bliss,
Nature scribbles, we can't resist.

In laughter's hues, the canvas swirls,
With whimsy written in petals and curls.
Spring's script unfolds, a playful spree,
Where every line elicits pure glee.

A Palette of Flora and Fantasy

In a garden realm where colors collide,
Butterflies giggle, on petals they glide.
A violet spills secrets in candy hues,
While poppies propose a dance—what a ruse!

A lily with glasses reads books in the sun,
Thinking it's clever, but no, it's just fun.
Dandelions puff up, trying to brag,
While tulips are stealing the scenery's flag.

With laughter as bright as the colors around,
The foliage whispers in jest, not a sound.
Each leaf a comedian, each stem in high glee,
Making us chuckle, just wait and see!

In this vibrant space, whimsy prevails,
Nature's own humor is painted in trails.
A palette of giggles, a fantasy bloom,
Where laughter and flowers always find room.

Pages Woven with Floral Dreams

On pages where daisies scribble delight,
Buttercups chuckle at a bird's silly flight.
With petals as ink, they plot and they scheme,
Drawing up sunlight into their grand dream.

A bookworm daffodil reads tales of the sun,
While roses recite their most fun pun.
Laughter echoes from vine-clad trees,
While bumbles play hopscotch with unsteady ease.

Snapdragons smirk with a magical grin,
As wind whispers jokes that make all hearts spin.
This literary garden is wild, full of cheer,
Floral pages of dreams that invite you near.

With each little verse, the humor does bloom,
In a tapestry woven, dispelling all gloom.
Lettuce giggles and tulips agree,
This book of blooms is the best cup of tea!

The Elegance of Written Flora

In gardens adorned with laughter's finesse,
Charming petals write with a playful bless.
Violets take notes on the jokes of the breeze,
While sun-kissed marigolds giggle with ease.

An azalea sways, penning tales of delight,
While gardenias blush at the stars of the night.
Foliage cracks wise as they bask in the sun,
Each little flower thinks they're the fun one.

With whimsy entwined in each vine and branch,
The flora unite in a grand laughter dance.
Each stem holds a secret, a punchline, a cheer,
Making the world just a bit more sincere.

Oh, the elegance found in their written grace,
Is a charming reminder of nature's embrace.
So let's celebrate jokes in the hue of the bloom,
For laughter, dear friend, is the best kind of room!

Tints of Nature's Verse

In the garden, words take flight,
Colorful phrases dance in light.
With each bloom, a pun appears,
Tickling laughs and lightened fears.

The daisies giggle, can you hear?
Jokes on leaves, let's grab a beer!
Tulips blushing, can't hold tight,
Watch out for the joke in flight.

In every corner, rhymes are found,
Whispers of humor lift from ground.
Nature's jest, a joyful scream,
Floating on a flowery dream.

Garden of Written Secrets

In secret corners, blooms conspire,
To hatch a tale that won't expire.
Lily pads with laughter float,
Joking frogs will steal the show.

Petunias penning sneaky notes,
Telling tales of naughty goats.
Sunflowers wink in bold array,
As bees write buzz in sunny play.

Behind the hedge, the humor grows,
Each stomp a pun that slowly shows.
With every bud, a joke it brings,
In flowers' laughter, nature sings.

The Symphony of Blooming Words

A symphony of colors bright,
Each note a giggle, pure delight.
Floral chords that dance and sway,
Playing tricks the funniest way.

Orchids gossip, tulips tease,
Nature's band plays tunes with ease.
Every stem a story told,
In petals' laughter, humor bold.

The lilacs hum in joyful rhymes,
Chasing squirrels through sunny climes.
Each blossom bursts with witty flair,
In this garden, jokes fill the air.

Strokes of Floral Imagination

In painter's hands, the colors dive,
Creating laughs that come alive.
Brushstrokes tickle every bud,
A canvas filled with joy and fun.

With swirls of green and flares of gold,
Each flower's tale is bright and bold.
Daffodils weave clever schemes,
In every petal, a giggle beams.

Violets doodle silly sights,
As roses wink at distant flights.
With each stroke, a jest unveiled,
In floral worlds, our dreams have sailed.

Strokes of Nature's Quill

In the garden, blooms do dance,
Their colors play, a quilt of chance.
With every breeze, a giggle hints,
As petals toss their floral prints.

Bees buzzing like a busy choir,
Conducting blooms with sweet desire.
They sip on nectar, oh so bold,
Leaving behind stories untold.

Sunshine paints with golden rays,
While shadows play in silly ways.
A flower's face, a cheeky grin,
Leaves trailing laughter in the wind.

The Garden's Written Secrets

Whispers bloom in vibrant hues,
Where roses tell their silly news.
With daisies giggling in a row,
Their secrets spread, just like the show.

Tulips jesting, take a bow,
As marigolds laugh, 'Oh, not now!'
They paint the scene with brush so neat,
Daily dramas, quite the treat!

Each leaf a letter, signed with glee,
Nature's post, for all to see.
In this book, no words are grim,
Just merry tales of whimsy's whim.

Tides of Blooming Imagination

Waves of petals, a colorful tide,
Float on laughter, nowhere to hide.
Each blossom dances in sunlight's beam,
Crafting a world, just like a dream.

A sunflower winks, a playful tease,
While violets giggle in the breeze.
They sway like puppets on a string,
In this garden, joy takes wing!

Laughter ripples through grassy fields,
With every secret that nature yields.
In every bloom, a story flows,
Nonsense and joy forever grows.

Ephemeral Leaves of Verse

Leaves flutter down with a comical flair,
Twirling around without a care.
Each one whispers a leafy joke,
Beneath the trees, the laughter spoke.

Grass blades giggle, tickled by feet,
As munching squirrels take a seat.
The winds carry tales of whimsy wide,
In nature's humor, we take pride.

With rhymes of roots and jingles of vine,
Each seed a punchline, how divine!
In this playful world where blooms converse,
Every leaf spins a colorful verse.

A Textured Tapestry of Nature's Words

In the garden of quirky thoughts,
Butterflies laugh at tangled knots.
Bumblebees hum a silly tune,
While daisies dance beneath the moon.

Squirrels debate in funny hats,
Telling tales of plump, fat cats.
Each blossom giggles with delight,
As sunbeams paint the world so bright.

Caterpillars write cheeky notes,
On soft petals, like tiny boats.
Nature's pen slips, spills some ink,
Creating art that makes you think.

Laughter blooms where flowers tread,
As crickets chirp and laugh instead.
In whispers of wind, tales unfold,
Of nature's humor, bright and bold.

Echoes of Nature's Breath

The trees chuckle in the breeze,
While ants practice their somersaults with ease.
A frog croaks jokes under the sun,
While petals giggle and have their fun.

Clouds play hide and seek at noon,
With shadows dancing to a tune.
The sun grins wide, it loves the show,
As laughter streams in bright green flow.

Each rustle tells a funny tale,
Of silly squirrels and wormy trails.
Nature's comedy, light and free,
Echoes forever, come join the spree.

With every breeze, a punchline flies,
Tickling the trees and the buzzing flies.
In this world of blooms and cheer,
Nature's humor, loud and clear.

Notes from the Secret Garden

In secret nooks where daisies peek,
Tomatoes gossip, oh so sweet.
Basil throws shade on sage so bright,
While onions snicker, quite a sight.

Vines climb high with acrobatic flair,
While snails race slowly, without a care.
The nightshade winks, a charming tease,
As whispers tickle the buzzing bees.

Rabbits wear coats, so dapper and neat,
While roses roll out a bold new beat.
Charming ivy sprawls with grace,
In this garden, every plant finds its place.

Lettuce leaps with a giggling grin,
While cucumbers share sweets from within.
In every leaf, a secret laid,
Nature's notes, perfectly played.

Flower-Laden Thoughts on Verses

In a meadow, thoughts take flight,
With flowers weaving words so bright.
Lilies snicker, daisies grin,
As whimsical verses now begin.

Tulips in hats play a grand charade,
While sunflowers pose, never afraid.
A garden gnome tells tales of jest,
As butterflies flitter, never rest.

Pansies chuckle, sharing dreams,
While dandelions float on sunny beams.
Nature's quips sprout like wild vines,
In every petal, laughter shines.

Each verse rolls like a playful wave,
In nature's book, the fun we crave.
So sip the sunshine, taste the cheer,
In this garden of giggles, draw near.

A Springtime Story in Stanzas

A book of blooms sits on the shelf,
With stories told by a lonely elf.
Tales of flowers that giggle and sway,
Turning pages as they laugh and play.

The daisies whisper jokes so funny,
While the sunflowers bask in the honey.
Each line a color, a fragrance light,
A springtime tale that brings delight.

Mushrooms wear hats, the leaves all cheer,
A raucous crowd, fill the atmosphere.
Ink spills laughter, giggling blooms roam,
In this silly garden, you feel at home.

We've captured joy in a vibrant hue,
Reading aloud beneath skies so blue.
With each turn, silliness does rise,
In this garden of quirk, we'll share the skies.

Enchanted Pages of Flora and Breeze

In a land where the daisies can dance,
Each flower winks, giving a chance.
The roses tell tales with a chuckle,
While tulips giggle, snorting and buckle.

A butterfly reads from a leaf of green,
Sharing secrets none have seen.
The breeze joins in with a mischievous sigh,
Spinning open the pages, oh my!

Petals whisper, 'What's more absurd?'
A gopher trying to read, have you heard?
He trips on rhymes, and the lilies laugh,
As the clouds drift by, taking their photograph.

Pages flutter like wild wings flying,
With flowers chortling and never sighing.
In colors of joy, the stories arise,
A funny world filled with bright surprise.

Ink and Leaf: A Dance of Color

Ink splats jump from the pen of a tree,
As leaves begin to dance with glee.
A vine tells stories that twist and shout,
Of bees in ballet with a buzzing route.

Each line a petal, a bubble of joy,
A worm with a tie, what a funny boy!
He recites haikus, wiggling about,
While cabbage rolls on, with a giggly shout.

A daisy holds court, with a crown of dew,
Making everyone laugh, both me and you.
Each page a riot of color and cheer,
As the flowers tell jokes loud and clear.

With every turn, the laughter is rife,
In the land of ink where plants have life.
A humorous world, alive and spry,
Where the colors of joy never say goodbye.

The Poetry of Wildflower Dreams

In a field of colors, a verse begins,
With wildflowers chortling, oh what a din!
A butterfly floats, a poetic sprite,
Reading aloud through day and night.

The poppies all giggle, tickled by sun,
As the violets plot silly pranks for fun.
Each stanza blooms under the sky so wide,
While the wind joins in, a memorable ride.

Roses snicker with tales of old,
Of garden gnomes who are cheeky and bold.
Ink drips laughter as petals relay,
The humor of nature in a bright display.

So flip through these pages, let joy abound,
Where every flower knows the humor found.
In this wacky world of colors and dreams,
Life's a funny poem, or so it seems.

Garden of Verses and Vivid Recollections

In a garden where words like weeds grow,
The daisies giggle, putting on a show.
Sunflowers wink from their lofty height,
While tulips gossip, oh what a sight!

The roses blush with a cheeky grin,
As bumblebees dance, they twirl and spin.
Petals play tricks like sneaky little spies,
Making hay fever cry with silly sighs!

Florals Dancing on the Pages

A daffodil waltzes, a silly old lass,
While marigolds giggle, letting time pass.
Orchids wear hats that are crooked and bright,
And violets tease with a flutter of light.

Each verse is a bud that starts to unfurl,
With ivy that whispers and starts to twirl.
The petals just laugh as the ink spills and flows,
Making baskets of joy wherever one goes!

Songs of the Blooming Quill

The quill sings sweetly with each little stroke,
While flowers laugh hard as they crack jokes.
Pansies parade with their colorful hats,
And daisies just roll like some floral acrobats.

Each line is a garden of whimsy and cheer,
As the tulips belt out tunes we all hear.
The ink drips in rhythm, a dance on the page,
Making each word feel as bright as the stage!

Threads of Eden's Dialogues

In Eden's embrace, the petals do chat,
"Why did the sunflower sit on the mat?"
The lilies all snicker, the lilies just play,
As they weave in and out, come along for the sway!

A rose with a wink utters puzzling jokes,
While clovers join in with some cheeky folks.
Each thread tells a tale that blossoms with glee,
In this garden of giggles, come share a cup of tea!

Floral Echoes Beneath the Ink

In a world where flowers write,
With colors bold, they take flight.
They scribble laughs on leafy sheets,
While bouncing blooms tap dancing beats.

The daisies giggle, tulips tease,
As sunbeams wear their summer fleas.
Petunias plot and pansies plan,
To sneak a snack from that big fat man.

Journals filled with fragrant tales,
Of sneaky bees and dancing snails.
They all conspire as flowers do,
To spread some joy in morning dew.

So grab your pens, let's write it down,
These floral jokes that spread around.
With every stroke, an echo rings,
In laughter's bloom, our hearts take wings.

The Blooming Songbook

A bouncy tune from roses bright,
Plays in gardens, pure delight.
With every note, a petal sways,
As daisies giggle through the haze.

The violets hum a merry tune,
While patchwork quilts of blooms attune.
They sing of bees in silly flights,
And ants that dance on starry nights.

Hummingbirds tap their tiny feet,
In rhythm where the blossoms meet.
The songs are sweet, the laughter loud,
In flowery fields, we join the crowd.

So grab your hats and join the spree,
With flowers laughing joyfully.
In every bloom, a note to glean,
Our funny songbook, bright and green.

Scripts in Nature's Palette

Nature pens a silly script,
With daisies heading every trip.
The trees are giggling at their shade,
As squirrel acrobats invade the glade.

On pages green, the bugs all write,
Of moonlit dances full of light.
The ants compose a marching band,
While bumblebees lend a helping hand.

Each line a laughing shade of fun,
With every blossom kissed by sun.
The grass scribbles jokes in the breeze,
While sunflowers bow to the teasing tease.

So join the dance, and don't delay,
In nature's script, we laugh and play.
With colors bright, the stories whirl,
Our funny scripts, a blooming pearl.

Tales of Verdant Whispers

Whispers weave through leaves so bright,
As flowers share their quirky light.
The lilacs gossip, tulips cheer,
While dandelions spread good cheer.

Their tales of spring are full of whim,
With butterflies that dance and swim.
The garden buzzes with chatter rife,
Of ladybugs finding their perfect life.

Each blade of grass has stories to spin,
Of clumsy frogs and their silly grin.
The violets snicker, the roses sing,
In nature's book, it's a blooming fling.

So listen close, let laughter flow,
In tales of green, we steal the show.
With every whisper, joy ignites,
In verdant laughter, our spirit light.

Heartstrings Tied with Violets

In gardens where the daisies dance,
A bee buzzed in its clumsy prance.
"Hey, flower! Want to join my show?"
"I'm busy! Go on, steal the show!"

Sunflowers laughed, their heads held high,
While roses pouted, oh my, oh my!
"Why do we let them take the lead?"
"Because we're fabulous, that's our creed!"

Butterflies flapped, in vibrant hues,
Winging opinions like the morning news.
"Who's that talking? Oh dear, not he!"
"Just a weed trying to steal our spree!"

But amidst the giggles, roots tangled tight,
Each bloom a story, each petal a light.
With laughter woven into their strings,
They sway and twirl, oh how joy sings!

The Chronicle of Botanical Whispers

In whispers soft, the lilacs share,
"Did you hear about the garden fair?"
"I wore a crown made of sturdy thyme,
But lost it all—what a silly crime!"

Tulips giggled, donned in their hues,
"Look at them scrambling, great reviews!"
"Roses with shoes? What a strange scene!"
"You should've seen them, like kings and queens!"

Dandelions puffed, their heads held high,
"Watch us float, just like clouds in the sky!"
The daisies rolled, in raucous cheer,
"You call that a whisper? We can't hear!"

Yet in the chaos, comes a wise bloom,
"Let's join the fun, dispel all gloom!"
For every laugh in the garden's heart,
Ties us together, that's just the start!

Lines Inked in Nature's Palette

With brushes made of leaves and dew,
The daisies painted their bright debut.
"Look at me! I'm a rainbow hue!"
"Aren't you mixed up? You've got no clue!"

The sunflowers grinned at their silly friends,
"We are the plot twist, where the fun bends!"
A squirrel sketched tales of acorn lore,
"Your lines are great, but mine must soar!"

In every corner, laughter would bloom,
As petals drafted their joyful room.
"Don't smudge the ink! We'll all turn grey!"
"But laughter's the color, come join our play!"

Under the sky, a canvas unfurled,
Where laughs and blooms created a world.
With cherry blossoms giggling so bright,
Ink spills of joy in the morning light!

Chapters of Blooms and Breezes

Pages turning, wind taking flight,
Every bloom has a story to write.
A tulip cried, "I'm the best in town!"
While violets giggled, "You're wearing a frown!"

The daisies chimed in, "What's that you say?"
"You might want to try a different display!"
Yet roses flaunted with petals so grand,
"We're the stars of this floral band!"

A bouncing butterfly skipped with glee,
"Let's turn this chapter into a spree!"
They danced on the breeze, with flair and style,
"It feels so great, let's giggle awhile!"

So here's to the tales of blooms that seem,
To blossom with laughter, to burst like a dream.
In the garden's grand book, pages unroll,
With humor the thread that weaves through it all!

Whispers of Blossom Ink

A flower wrote a letter, quite absurd,
It said, 'Stop being thorny!' how it stirred.
In a garden where giggles take flight,
Even daisies crack jokes 'til night.

With petals as paper, they'll compose,
Silly sonnets about garden gnomes.
Bees buzz in rhythm, a quirky tune,
Chasing butterflies 'neath a smiling moon.

Each stem, a story, each bud, a jest,
Nature's comedy club, simply the best!
As roses reenact a blooper reel,
Laughter's the nectar, oh what a deal!

So if you hear whispers, don't be coy,
It's just the blooms giggling with joy!
Grab a daffodil, have a laugh, too,
In this floral farce, there's fun for you!

The Blooming Narrative

In the garden of giggles, all is bright,
Sunflowers gossip and delight.
Tulips wear hats, it's a fashion spree,
While violets tango under the tree.

A rose tells a tale of love gone wrong,
Its thorns were cruel, it sang a sad song.
But lilies chime in with a dance so grand,
Spinning tales of romance, oh so planned!

Every petal bears witness to fun,
From busted vines to playful runs.
They laugh at the bees with clumsy ways,
As pollen clouds generate sunny rays.

So join this bloom tale, come take a seat,
Where stories of flowers are ever sweet!
In this patch of whimsy, let's all unite,
For laughter's the flower that blooms in delight!

Leaves of Colorful Dreams

In a dream where leaves wore shoes,
They danced round petals, chasing blues.
Swaying with laughter, a leafy parade,
How they chuckled at blades of grass, unafraid!

Acorns telling jokes about falling down,
While bumblebees prance through the town.
Each leaf has a punchline; it's quite absurd,
Dancing with joy as the sun's warmth stirred.

The trees get tipsy on sweet morning dew,
Sipping on rainbows, just two and a few.
With branches flailing to rhythm divine,
They giggle and sway, oh, what a fine line!

So when you walk through this leafy space,
Look closely for smiles on nature's face.
In every flutter, find laughter's gleam,
As leaves whisper secrets of colorful dreams!

Flora's Ephemeral Stories

In a book made of blooms, stories unfold,
With tales of butterflies, both brave and bold.
A daisy tripped over her charming rhyme,
As ferns laughed so hard, they lost track of time.

Every blossom's a character, colorful and sly,
Petunias plot mischief as bumblebees fly.
A carnation, the critic, with petals to spare,
Rating each giggle with a sophisticated air.

In this story garden, all is quite bright,
Where tulips play chess under the moonlight.
With each passing breeze, a new page is turned,
As flora spins yarns, oh, how they yearn!

So dive into laughter, it's hard to contain,
In Flora's tales, there's no room for pain.
With leaf-turning antics, adventures so grand,
Join the blooms as they jive, hand in hand!

Petals Beneath a Sky of Ink

In gardens where the colors clash,
The flowers giggle, making a splash.
Bumblebees wear tiny hats,
Sipping nectar, sharing chats.

A daffodil thinks it looks quite grand,
While the tulip's doing a silly stand.
Roses play hide and seek with the sun,
Every day is a blooming fun run.

The daisies peek from a leafy shroud,
Waving proudly, feeling quite loud.
Their laughter dances in the breeze,
Making even the dullest hearts tease.

And when the sky spills its inky hue,
The flowers prance, it's their favorite view.
With petals swaying to the night's sweet song,
In this garden, nothing feels wrong.

Inked Horizons of Floral Delight

A sunflower stretched its neck so high,
Claiming it's best, and giving a sigh.
Across the field, a clumsy bee,
Buzzing around like it's lost at sea.

The violets joke about a breeze,
That tickles their leaves and brings them ease.
While the lilies roll their eyes in glee,
Saying, "We're the stars, can't you see?"

A tiny bud decided to dance,
Spinning in circles, taking a chance.
All the roses joined in the fun,
With laughter echoing, second to none.

Under the vast, ink-black sky,
They paint the night without a shy.
With colors swirling and hearts so bright,
These blossoms bloom, what a magical sight!

The Sonnet of Swaying Blooms

A daisy writes a whimsical rhyme,
Claiming the best title of all time.
With petals outstretched, it takes the stage,
As the breeze flips through its leafy page.

Lilacs giggle at the silly humor,
While daisies dance with clouds of rumor.
Caught in a twirl, a tulip slips,
Making the wind giggle with its flippy tips.

Each flower waves like a jolly cheer,
As night falls, they don their party gear.
With moonlit laughs and twinkling eyes,
They sway and swing beneath the starry skies.

So let's toast to blooms under the gleam,
In this garden where flowers dream.
With inked horizons and laughter's tone,
Each petal's a page in nature's own tome.

Blossoms of Solace and Sorrow

A reluctant rose shed its age-old tears,
Saying, "Hey, life's not all cheers!"
But violets chimed in, "Stay awhile!
Let's share our woes with a floral smile!"

The pansies grinned, "Don't fret, dear friend,
Every thorn has a soft little end!"
With petals that glimmer in moonlit glow,
They danced away sorrows, putting on a show.

Sunflowers turned, their faces aglow,
Whispering secrets in winds that flow.
"Together," they laughed, "we make quite a pair,
In sorrow and solace, we bloom with flair!"

So when the ink drips down from the sky,
The blossoms giggle, wipe tears dry.
With humor stitched in their fragrant song,
In this tapestry of life, they all belong.

The Verses of Petal and Stem

In a garden of giggles, flowers convene,
They hold secret parties, if you know what I mean.
The daisies are dancing, the roses all jest,
While sunflowers gossip, they'd win any quest.

Bees bring the snacks, all honey and cheer,
The butterflies flutter, they spread joy, never fear.
Worms are the bouncers, so sly and so spry,
"No slithering in here, or you'll surely fly by!"

Come join in the laughter, the fun never ends,
Where blooms make you chuckle, and petals befriend.
In this leafy oasis, where whimsy takes flight,
The garden will giggle from morning to night.

So tiptoe through blooms, don't make a loud sound,
Or the giggling tulips might just pitch you outta town!
Laughter is plentiful, in this floral delight,
In the realm of the garden, it's a silly sight!

Chronicles in the Shade of Blossoms

Under leafy umbrellas, stories unfold,
Of violets with secrets, all shy but bold.
They whisper of squirrels, the antics they play,
As daisies roll over and giggle all day.

The moon seen peeking, a mischievous sprite,
Spinning wild tales of the dance last night.
The lilies are laughing, with jokes up their sleeves,
While nettles stand guard, like sentry on leaves.

Pansies wear costumes, they've dressed up for fun,
While hedgehogs tell tales of their wild, moonlit runs.
How dandelions tamed a storm just for show,
And what really happens when garden gnomes glow.

So gather 'round petals, let stories collide,
In a world filled with giggles, where joy takes a ride.
The blossoms will sing, of laughter and glee,
In the shade of the blossoms, come share it with me!

Whims of the Garden's Heart

In the heart of the garden, where sunlight reveals,
A turkey is strutting, wearing high heels.
The flowers are snickering, hushed huffs in the breeze,
As frogs hop along, spitting out jokes with ease.

From clover's bright patches, to roots underground,
Worms share the latest, news flying around.
"Last week, I saw, a rabbit that danced,
With daisies around him, they giggled and pranced!"

With butterflies fluttering, all painted with flair,
They color the skies with laughter to share.
"Have you heard that old tale, of bees in a band?
They buzzed out a tune, and the lilies all fanned!"

So join in the frolic, let silliness sway,
The charm of the blooms, will brighten your day.
In the garden's warm embrace, we laugh and we tease,
Where whimsy is found, you'll find joy with ease!

Flora's Story Told in Shades

Among the bright petals, a drama unfolds,
With snorting hyacinths, and sunflowers bold.
They gather 'round gossiping, silly and spry,
As violets snicker, "Did you see that? Oh my!"

The laughter erupts, like rain on hot ground,
As tulips trade stories, of magic they found.
With whispers of ladybugs, who love to play tricks,
And jolly old bumblebees, pulling quick flicks.

The grasses are swaying, to a whimsical beat,
As daisies jump in, with their two-left feet.
They spin in a circle, and tumble with glee,
In this garden of laughter, forever carefree.

From roses to poppies, they join in the fun,
With playful enchantments, and laughter spun.
So swing by the flowers, where silliness thrives,
In a tale of the flora, where humor survives!

www.ingramcontent.com/pod-product-compliance
Lightning Source LLC
Chambersburg PA
CBHW072143200426
43209CB00051B/305